Operational Decision Management FOR DUMMIES

A Wiley Brand

IBM Limited Edition

by Steve Craggs and Brian Safron

FOR DUMMIES
A Wiley Brand

Operational Decision Management For Dummies®, IBM Limited Edition

Published by
John Wiley & Sons, Inc.
111 River St.
Hoboken, NJ 07030-5774
www.wiley.com

Published by John Wiley & Sons, Inc., Hoboken, New Jersey

For general information on our other products and services, or how to create a custom *For Dummies* book for your business or organization, please contact our Business Development Department in the U.S. at 877-409-4177, contact info@dummies.biz, or visit www.wiley.com/go/custompub. For information about licensing the *For Dummies* brand for products or services, contact BrandedRights&Licenses@Wiley.com.

ISBN 978-1-118-67957-9 (pbk); ISBN 978-1-118-67978-4 (ebk)

Manufactured in the United States of America

10 9 8 7 6 5 4 3 2 1

Table of Contents

Publisher's Acknowledgments

We're proud of this book and of the people who worked on it. For details on how to create a custom *For Dummies* book for your business or organization, contact `info@dummies.biz` or visit `www.wiley.com/go/custompub`. For details on licensing the *For Dummies* brand for products or services, contact `BrandedRights&Licenses@Wiley.com`.

Some of the people who helped bring this book to market include the following:

Acquisitions, Editorial, and Media Development

Project Editor: Carrie A. Burchfield

Editorial Manager: Rev Mengle

Business Development Representative: Sue Blessing

Custom Publishing Project Specialist: Michael Sullivan

Composition Services

Senior Project Coordinator: Kristie Rees

Layout and Graphics: Sean Decker

Proofreader: Susan Moritz

Publishing and Editorial for Technology Dummies

Richard Swadley, Vice President and Executive Group Publisher

Andy Cummings, Vice President and Publisher

Mary Bednarek, Executive Director, Acquisitions

Mary C. Corder, Editorial Director

Publishing and Editorial for Consumer Dummies

Kathleen Nebenhaus, Vice President and Executive Publisher

Composition Services

Debbie Stailey, Director of Composition Services

Business Development

Lisa Coleman, Director, New Market and Brand Development

Introduction

Does any of this sound familiar?

- Your business rules are hidden in your applications or processes (and are hard to find and change).
- You'd like to automate your operational decisions, assuming the solution was safe and reliable.
- The system used to manage your business rules is hard to use and isn't accessible by your business experts.
- IT is so backlogged that change requests often take months to implement.

If so, Operational Decision Management (ODM) may be just what you need.

ODM is the evolution of business rules management. It provides a complete, easy-to-use system for automating day-to-day operational decisions and allows businesspeople and IT to collaborate on business rules by using an interface and a language that are comfortable and intuitive for both.

Simply put, ODM is about change. If rules and decisions don't ever need to change, there's probably no need to put them in an ODM system. But for rules that *do* change (rules that control pricing, eligibility, credit approvals, claims processing, and so on), ODM offers a proven solution to manage that change.

ODM not only allows you to automate your business rules, but also it enables you to detect real-time business events (such as a person making a credit card charge) and use rules to decide and automate the appropriate response or action to those events.

About This Book

This book is written for readers who have varying levels of familiarity with ODM. It doesn't focus on any particular vendor's offering; instead, it talks about the features of ODM as a model for managing operational decision-making.

This book isn't about offline business intelligence systems. While those systems are very valuable, the focus of this book is on automated decisions that can be executed in real time in conjunction with your business applications and processes.

Conventions Used in This Book

Because ODM is for everyone, not just the IT department, we use the term *business user* to differentiate employees who don't work in IT from those who do. Business users may be business or operational analysts, managers, process designers, and so on.

Icons Used in This Book

You'll find these icons in the margins of this book:

TIP

The Tip icon points out time- or frustration-saving ideas.

REMEMBER

The Remember icon marks information that you should take from the discussion and file away in your brain, even if you remember nothing else.

TECHNICAL STUFF

This icon highlights information that you don't need to know but may find interesting.

WARNING!

Pay close attention to anything that has a Warning icon. Failure to heed this information could have serious consequences for your business.

Chapter 1

What Is Operational Decision Management?

In This Chapter

- Managing your business by managing your decisions
- Organizing business rules

Operational decision management (ODM) is a set of technologies and methods that allow you to automate your day-to-day business decisions without compromising their accuracy and effectiveness. ODM lets you document, implement, change, and govern the repeatable decisions that control your business operations. It combines a system for managing business rules with a business rules engine to deliver agility and control in your day-to-day operations. More to the point, ODM is about making change easier and extending change control to business users who are responsible for the business policies, regulations, and practices that run your business.

In this chapter, we give you a broad overview of ODM.

Controlling the Decisions That Control Your Business

Everything your business does relies on decisions. You have to decide what rate to charge a client, for example, and which supplier to use, as well as when to reorder stock and make a specific investment. It's fair to say that decisions control your business.

But who controls those decisions?

Think about your own organization. Perhaps you have decisions embedded in the applications that run your business, maybe you rely on skilled staff members to make the right decisions, or you may explain the decision-making you want in corporate memos or an employee policy document. In short, your repeatable decisions may be scattered across a range of sources (some automated and some manual) with no guarantee of consistency, and changing any of them can be a real headache. This is where ODM comes in.

Seeing how decisions are managed

The problem of handling a mishmash of decision-making processes is precisely what decision management is designed to solve. It encompasses the tools and methods you need to gather your decisions together and manage any changes efficiently, effectively, and safely.

The decision management process involves three steps:

1. **Extract the decision-making logic from wherever it resides today (such as an application, business process, spreadsheet, policy manual, or someone's brain).**
2. **Put the decisions in a library so you can search for them to find the ones you want.**
3. **Provide a way for people to view, edit, model, and deploy new changes.**

In short, decision management creates order from chaos.

You can ensure responsible governance by using decision management tools to assure proper decision approval, secure the library, provide authorization for changes, measure decision outcomes, and create a feedback loop to identify further improvements and refinements. What you get back are decisions that are consistent, predictable, verifiable, and efficient.

Putting the "operational" in ODM

Now that you know what decision management can do for your decisions, you may be asking about the purpose of the *operational* part of ODM. You may wonder whether that word is redundant, added just to make the subject sound more mysterious. It isn't, as we show you in this section.

The decisions that run any business are often described as falling into two categories:

- **Strategic decisions:** Strategic decisions are important decisions that affect the future of your business, such as whether to start selling your products in China or whether to source more components locally. These decisions are likely to be made over a long period and take considerable thought and effort.
- **Operational decisions:** Operational decisions, by contrast, are repeatable decisions made as part of day-to-day business operations. These decisions happen in real time, as business interactions are being executed, and they control the next step of the business process or deliver the final process outcome. Typically, you don't have time to think about them, and, unlike strategic decisions, they're good candidates for automation.

These operational decisions can have a massive effect on your business performance. Because they're often executed many thousands of times a day, they can make the difference between success and failure. So you need these decisions to be accurate and predictable. Managing them properly is essential.

Enter ODM.

Managing Decisions with ODM

ODM offers more than just a way to automate repeatable decisions. It provides a management system to make sure that the decisions are consistent and correct. These decisions are the virtual equivalent of levers and buttons that you can pull or press to change your operational execution.

Imagine that you run an online fashion boutique, and you're hoping for a surge in sales as all those fashion-conscious teenagers get ready for the new school year. Your daughter, however, tells you that she just ordered three new outfits from a competitor that's running a special back-to-school promotion: 10 percent off a purchase of three or more items. If only you had a way to change your business applications to make a competitive offer before any more damage is done . . .

Wait — ODM saves the day! Just change the decision on your billing discount to include a 15 percent discount for orders of three or more items.

The real beauty of using your decisions to manage your business this way is that you don't need to look at the whole process of selling clothes and accessories online. You don't need to check the way the process works, ask for new code to be written, or distribute an urgent memo to the call-center staff. You just find the discount-rate criteria and change them.

REMEMBER

Part of managing your decisions, however, is looking at the impact of any changes. In reality, you may not want to make your new "15 percent off three or more items" offer just to get the teenage back-to-school business. After all, cornering the market and making a loss on each transaction may not be a recipe for great success.

TIP

You may want to run your proposed deal against your sales for the same back-to-school period last year to see what it would have done to your profitability then. The new offer might increase your volume, but is that increase enough to make it worthwhile? Managing your decisions lets you manage your business carefully.

Writing Your Decisions Down: Business Rules

After a while, it gets rather tedious to talk about the record of how a business decision is made; you need a shorthand way to notate business decisions. That's the role of business rules, usually called just *rules*.

Key rules written down in business terms are valuable assets in themselves. They become visible to the entire organization, offering a single source of the truth for how business policies are executed in your business systems.

We cover rules in detail in Chapter 4. Here, we briefly show you how rules work with ODM.

Finding a format for rules

Rules are written in nontechnical terms so that they can be written, viewed, and edited by average business users. Some rules may be in a natural-language form, such as these examples:

> IF car is 4wd AND applicant is under 21 yrs old THEN add 30% to the insurance premium
>
> IF customer level = platinum THEN discount = 15%

Other rules are in some other business-accessible form, such as a spreadsheet–like decision table setting out rates against vehicle sizes and age ranges, or a list of countries and their corresponding shipment surcharges.

Managing rules and events with ODM

ODM is the evolution of business rules management. The technology was designed to simplify the process of creating, managing, changing, and governing the rules that represent the inner workings of a business. Some organizations use ODM to manage several hundred rules; others use it to manage thousands or tens of thousands of rules. ODM is designed to create and execute virtually any number of rules with high performance.

ODM can also capture patterns of real-time business events (such as a single person making withdrawals within a 15-minute period from two bank machines that are 1,000 miles apart), analyzing those events, and using rules to determine the appropriate action.

In ODM, business rules are written in plain language, not in computer code (refer to "Finding a format for rules," earlier in this chapter), and businesspeople can make most of the day-to-day changes to those rules.

As you see throughout the book, the ability to make changes quickly yet safely is central to ODM. Although many organizations spend a lot of time talking about how to align business and IT, ODM is a tangible way to make that alignment real.

Grouping rules with ODM

If you think about one of your processes, you can probably spot many decisions that control it. If each of these decisions is a rule, you could have thousands of rules. How will you ever find the one you want?

One way is through a searchable rules repository. Current technology makes it relatively easy to find any rule based on search parameters. So even if you don't remember which folder contains a certain rule, you can use search features to quickly find the rule you're looking for.

The decision management answer is to group related rules so that they're easier to find (but don't worry; if a rule's hard to find, you can always use the search function). Imagine a library, which has sections so that you can quickly find the book you want. Your business "library" might have pricing rules for household goods in one bookcase, for example, with rules for individual appliances on each shelf. The idea is to make the organization intuitive and helpful for your employees so they can store the rules in the right place so others can find them later.

Chapter 2

Is ODM Right for You?

In This Chapter

- Considering the benefits of ODM
- Seeing how ODM might help your business

Before giving any more attention to ODM, you may want to sort out whether it's worth the bother. (After all, if you don't feel you're going to get any returns from ODM, reading the rest of this book seems pointless, doesn't it?) If so, this chapter is for you.

Seeing What ODM Can Do for You

Can ODM really help you automate your real-time decisions in a precise and consistent way? Can it deliver on the promise of allowing your business users to quickly yet safely make changes to your business rules?

The value of ODM comes from extracting the business rules that control your operations from wherever they're stored, documenting them in clear, concise form, and then providing tools that allow you to review, analyze, model, edit, and deploy them to meet your dynamic business needs.

TIP

ODM provides a wide range of benefits:

- **Enabling rapid and agile change:** Your employees can write and edit your operational decisions as needed, perhaps in collaboration with other departments, to ensure that the business can react quickly to both opportunities and threats.

Also, operational change can be made quickly and directly by business experts, which eliminates any application-development backlog.

- **Capturing the knowledge of your experts for reuse:** Your automated systems can perform like your experts, making decisions based on the experience and expertise or your best and most-experienced employees.
- **Ensuring consistency:** ODM makes operational decisions predictable and repeatable.
- **Refining and updating decisions:** You can model, measure, collaborate on, and refine your decisions to keep up with the needs of your business.
- **Facilitating compliance:** ODM provides a clear record of the rules governing business operations, enabling greater collaboration and more effective compliance management. Decisions are documented in nontechnical language, and you can review them at any time, making sure that they fit with corporate and regulatory policies.
- **Improving customer service:** ODM makes your customer service not only personalized and high quality but also consistent, based on accurate, repeatable, rules-based decisions.

We discuss these benefits in more detail in the following sections.

Enabling rapid and agile change

Competition is cutthroat. Companies must not only try to maintain market share but also push to find new markets and customers. If you want to win in this dynamic and fast-moving environment, you have to be agile enough to stay ahead of the pack.

It can be hard work for your employees to turn their ideas into reality, especially when they have to request changes through the overworked IT department. ODM, however, puts the power of change into your employees' hands, allowing them to collaborate with IT and bypass cumbersome application-development queues. Some rules in ODM are written in plain language, and others are expressed in spreadsheet-like decision tables (see Chapter 1), but all are in a form that your employees can understand. The ODM tools help them simulate and validate any changes to rules before deploying the changes. Businesspeople can safely model, govern, and enact changes with minimal need to bother IT.

Any operational change that you make to catch a wave in the market or to tackle a growing threat has to start with your business teams. The business analysts are the ones who have their fingers on the pulse of the market, detecting any changes and thinking of ways to seize the initiative.

Capturing the knowledge of your experts for reuse

Have you ever had a superstar in your company who's at least a demigod in her field? This expert is involved in all the biggest and most important deals because she's done it all before and knows the business like the back of her hand. If only you had a department full of clones of that expert, you could always give the same response to a customer, always make the optimum offer to a buyer, and always know the right way to settle a claim with a policyholder.

Most companies don't work that way, however. Employees' skill levels vary, and they don't always have time to ask an internal expert for advice. Nothing can make up for lack of experience. ODM is designed to get that vital information out of your experts' heads and into repeatable, automatable rules.

Ensuring consistency

ODM rules always produce predictable, repeatable results. Rules don't have off days, they don't make mistakes, they don't get upset, and they execute your operational decisions the same way every time. This consistency is good for the accuracy and predictability of your business operations, and it's great for your customers and partners.

Consistency creates value throughout your operations. Making repeatable *and* accurate decisions consistently can increase your sales, maximize your profits, and improve customer satisfaction and retention.

Refining and updating decisions

Business leaders love ODM because it helps them measure the outcomes of critical operational decisions. If you discover that your rule will result in 80 percent exceptions, for example, the rule won't achieve what you want. If this rule causes delays for your customers, you may want to look at the conditions under which decisions are being referred to see whether you can relax the rule without harming operations.

TIP

Being able to simulate and measure decision outcomes provides important input on how your business is running and gives you the information you need to improve efficiency and effectiveness.

Facilitating compliance

Compliance officers love ODM. When the rules controlling business operations are documented in understandable terms, it's much easier to check them against corporate policies and external regulations. ODM also enables the compliance officer to generate reports and keep an eye on compliance status without bothering your business users. Because rules are nontechnical and easy to understand, he or she can search the rules library and check sensitive rules without having to ask for help.

Improving customer service

With ODM your automated systems can provide personalized customer service. Your business rules can take into account everything you know about each customer to personalize your service. For example, you may not want to send an e-mail offer to a customer for a product he purchased from you last week. Or you may want to offer different banking products to each customer depending on his average account balance, number of accounts, and credit history.

Also, a great irritation for customers is getting different answers to the same enquiry. The consistency delivered by applying ODM to decision-making ensures that you'll always give the same response, which builds customer confidence and satisfaction. Also, because ODM-managed decisions are based on shared rules, as these rules improve and become more accurate, all decisions using these rules will benefit, raising overall quality of service.

Solving Your Decision Problems with ODM

As we discuss throughout the book, rules are just mechanisms for expressing how a business operates and for enabling the business to change fast enough (but in a governed way) to keep up with the evolving business and regulatory environments. ODM is fundamentally about enabling business precision and change.

How do you know whether ODM can bring that precision to your business? Here are a few key problems that ODM may be able to help you solve.

Long, slow change cycle

If it takes too long to implement changes to your business policies, ODM may be a solution.

How long is "too long" varies from business to business, of course. In our experience, most organizations with hundreds or thousands of business rules would like to implement changes in some of those rules on a weekly or perhaps monthly basis. But we've also found that it takes many organizations six to eight months to implement rule changes (with full governance, of course).

Complex decision code

Code is great for structuring how an application performs its tasks, but it's not as good for communicating business policies. In many instances, the outcome intended by the business unit isn't what was coded into the IT applications.

ODM simplifies rules by describing business policies and regulations in easy-to-read language, which has an important added benefit: IT users also can easily read and understand the intent of a rule. With as much as they have on their plates these days, IT users typically don't have the time to learn to read multiple languages and applications. If you want everybody to interpret business rules the same way, it makes sense to describe those rules in simple language that everybody in the company can read.

Need for more straight-through processing

Anything that can be automated (effectively, of course) should be automated. We all want to free people to do the things that people do best, which means that computers should do what computers do best. The benefits that can come from increasing straight-through processing by just a few percentage points are enormous. For example, the improvement from automating 85 percent of eligibility decisions, compared to say 75 percent, can mean millions of dollars of profit and greatly improved customer satisfaction.

In the past, one of the greatest obstacles to achieving higher rates of straight-through processing was that computer systems couldn't make the fine-grained decisions that human experts could. ODM makes that situation somewhat obsolete. As more and more routine decisions can be made without human intervention, your straight-through processing will increase (and so will your profits).

Hard-to-find decision criteria

It comes as no surprise that decision criteria were traditionally hard-coded into applications. In a sense, that's what applications were for: to automate business logic. When changing business rules once a year was acceptable practice, the situation was fine. Today, however, the pace of business is much faster, rolling out a new version of an application is harder, and although development has gotten faster and more agile, most applications can't be updated on a weekly, or even monthly, basis.

If you keep your business rules separate from your applications, you can have the best of both worlds. With ODM, applications can be updated on a sustainable timeline, and business rules can be updated at the speed of business.

Overworked IT staff

Ever since the tech bubble burst in the early 2000s, IT resources have been more heavily scrutinized, and IT departments have been asked to do a lot more with a lot less. ODM, however, creates a win-win situation for business and IT. Businesspeople can make the ongoing changes in business rules, and IT can own the business rules application and ensure its integrity and performance. This perfect division of labor lets everybody do what he or she is best at.

Miscommunicated change requests

In the past, you may have asked for a change and spelled out exactly what that change should be. After several months of work, IT finally implemented the change . . . and it wasn't what you intended. You may have tried to identify the source of the miscommunication, but you probably couldn't stop the situation from happening again.

Mind you, many business analysts working in IT understand the business well enough to implement what the business intended — but not enough of them to prevent the inevitable fumbles that take place in the handoff. ODM provides a safe and governed environment in which business users can create and update business rules directly, without relying on IT, thus eliminating (or at least significantly reducing) miscommunication.

No clear audit history

You've probably seen the classic interrogation scene in crime movies. The police ask something like "Where were you on the night of June 17?" The suspect fakes a look of dismay and protests that it's impossible to remember a specific night six months ago.

Although they probably aren't guilty of lawbreaking, applications are no different from the suspects in those movies. They don't have easily accessible memories of all the transactions that were executed on any given date or of the specific rules that were in place at the time of those transactions. Suppose that a loan was denied on July 1, and three months later, you need to provide proof that the loan was rejected based on company policy. Can you easily audit the computer system that made the decision to determine the specific, quantifiable reason for the rejection and the criteria that were used?

TIP

With ODM, you get a complete, easily accessible audit trail that lets you trace your decision history throughout the lifetime of the application.

Chapter 3

Looking under ODM's Hood

In This Chapter

- Viewing the components of an ODM system
- Making the system user-friendly
- Ensuring security

If you've decided that ODM is for you (perhaps as a result of reading Chapter 2), you're going to need to know what goes in an ODM system. This chapter pops the hood to give you a look.

The Anatomy of an ODM Solution

Figure 3-1 shows the key components of an ODM solution and how they relate to one another.

These components are

- *The rules library,* an organized repository for all your rules
- *Developer tools* for setting up your rules environment and maintaining your rules application
- *Rules and events management tools* for browsing, viewing, editing, saving, modeling, testing, governing, and deploying new and modified rules
- A *runtime engine* that executes your rules within your operational environment as required

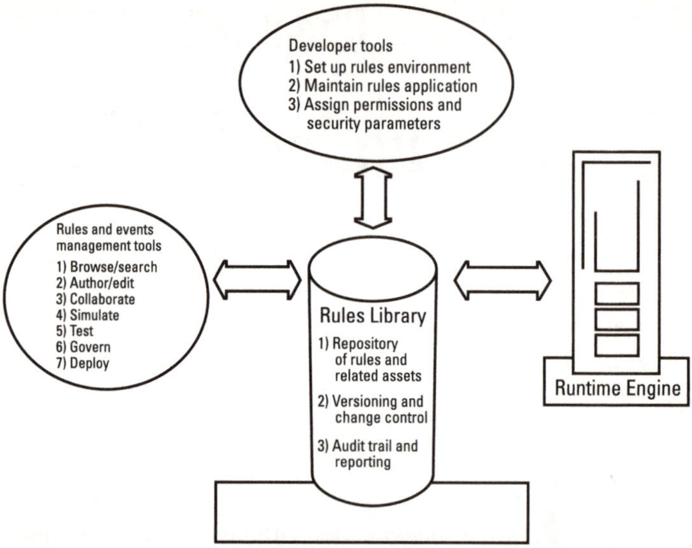

Figure 3-1: The components of an ODM system.

Rules and events management tools

To get the best bang for your ODM buck, you need to liberate your business users to respond quickly and accurately to market changes and opportunities. If you expect your business users to change how business operations work on their own, however, you have to make sure that they're comfortable enough with the tools to make changes with confidence. (We discuss user comfort further in "Making ODM User-Friendly," later in this chapter.) For this reason, ODM products make business user tools a priority, and IT users also benefit from this ease of use.

Rules generally follow one of two simple formats (see Chapter 1), depending on what sorts of decisions they're designed to address. Also, ODM products provide test and simulation tools to help business users deliver higher-quality results, as well as a full range of governance tools to ensure the right approvals are in place before deploying any rule.

Users must have the correct authority and approvals before deploying any rule changes, of course. Governance is a key facet of ODM.

Developer tools

ODM developer tools set up the environment in such a way that the business users can use it without seeing the hidden complexity. The art of ODM is letting developers deal with all the tricky stuff, leaving business users free to concentrate on doing what the business needs when it needs it.

Developers create the environment for business users in various ways, such as defining or importing data models, defining the names that can be part of a rule expression (such as customer number, zip code, or product type), specifying how these names relate to actual system variables, and specifying how the rules engine will invoke them when necessary.

Making ODM User-Friendly

The IT industry is good at tackling technical problems, but it's always found a greater challenge in talking to business users. IT personnel consistently misjudge how hostile technological solutions can seem to nontechnical people. Even something as simple to developers as an explorer-style library tree structure may be unfamiliar to business users.

If you want your business users to take advantage of the power of ODM by writing and changing the rules that control business operations, you have to go beyond just not scaring them with IT procedures and terminology. You need to empower business users so that they're comfortable with the ODM rule-authoring tools and confident in their ability to make the changes the business needs.

ODM products provide a range of tools and environments designed to make business users feel at home, such as the following features:

- Business-oriented browse/search facilities for navigating the rules library

- Documentation or contact information for rules
- Access to the ODM system from Microsoft Office products such as Word and Excel
- Collaboration tools that enable users to discuss possible changes and get advice
- Simulation tools for checking out the effect of a proposed change

We discuss some of these features in the following sections.

Navigation search support

The Internet has changed us all; it's second nature now to look up information in search engines. Business users are no different. If they can't find the rules and related information they need, they won't be able to make the changes required.

ODM tools provide lots of support for navigating the rules library. Using these tools feels as natural as surfing the web at home, which is important: As soon as users start to feel that things are getting too technical, their confidence falls. Providing easy-to-use search features and plug-ins for popular business environments such as Microsoft Office goes a long way toward making the procedure less scary.

Imagine that your U.S. mail-order firm ships a range of books to many locations throughout the world and that management just decided to waive the cost of shipping books domestically. Business users will want to surf the rules library, looking for rules governing delivery costs. When they find the right section, they probably want to see whether specific rules already exist for domestic shipments and/or nondigital books.

After the users find the right rules, they may want help finding supporting information. They can easily use the ODM system to search for documentation and review change histories.

Collaboration

One of the best ways to build confidence and accuracy is to be able to share your thoughts with others. ODM allows business users to discuss and collaborate on proposed rule changes, which ensures that rules are high quality, are based on pooled experience, and also empower users to make the necessary changes without fear.

Your business users will take advantage of opportunities to collaborate only if the collaboration tools are easy to use and intuitive. Therefore, ODM tools work hard to provide business users the sort of collaboration environments that they may use in their personal lives.

Testing and validation

Simple rule changes and their consequences may seem obvious, but are you really prepared to risk your business operations based on something that *seems* obvious? ODM is designed to make business operations work consistently and accurately, so it's no surprise that ODM products provide tools that help with testing and validating proposed rule changes.

One of the most valuable features allows users to simulate the new changes and see what would happen, usually by building sample data for the rules to work from or by running a simulation against historical operational data. By simulating the new rules and reporting on the results, your users can identify and fix any unwanted effects and then move forward with the changes with greater confidence.

Ensuring security

Although ODM makes it easier to make changes to business rules, never forget that these rules control the operational decisions being made inside your company hundreds or thousands of times a day. Yes, the power to adjust operations quickly to take advantage of new opportunities or combat new threats is valuable, but uncontrolled change could have serious repercussions on your business activities.

Therefore, ODM products provide security and authorization mechanisms so that you always know who has the power to make specific changes and what approval procedures are in place for those changes.

Chapter 4

The Life Cycle of Rules

In This Chapter

- Getting an overview of rules
- Understanding how business rules work
- Seeing how rules are made

Managing your decisions wisely helps you manage your business wisely, and to do that you need rules, which are simply your operational decision-making criteria written down so they can be automated in real time. In this chapter, we walk you through the life cycle of rules in ODM.

Taking a Wider View of Rules

Rules that control operational decisions usually relate to parts of the business interaction being executed. When an insurance eligibility decision needs to be made in the course of a claims process, for example, a rule clicks in, and the approval or denial is registered into the process. (Of course, sometimes the decision results in an exception that must be handled manually, but rules are also good for identifying those exceptions.) Sometimes, however, you need to do things a different way.

Instead of invoking a rule as part of a particular business transaction execution, you may want to trigger it based on some sort of external event. Maybe you want to automatically reassign the stores to which your warehouse ships your inventory based on real-time weather patterns, or perhaps you want to take some action when a credit card is swiped or a particular section of your website is visited or clicked.

ODM systems typically incorporate support for event-driven rules as well as the more common transaction-driven approach.

Seeing How Business Rules Work

In this section, we use a slightly trivial example to illustrate how business rules work.

Writing a simple rule

Suppose that you want to decide whether to go to the ballgame this weekend with your significant other. You might write a rule that states the following:

> IF 2 adjacent tickets are available to the game in section 103, 104, or 105 for less than $50 per ticket
>
> AND IF no relatives are visiting on the day of the game
>
> AND IF the low temperature on the day of the game is not less than 40°F
>
> THEN buy tickets to the game

You may wonder why you'd use a computer system to make such a simple decision. The answer is simple. You can make a decision like this in your head, or in a spreadsheet program, if you're making it only once a week. But if you're making 1,000 decisions a day based on 100 rules — or 10,000 decisions based on 1,000 rules — you need some high-tech help.

You may have this type of decision logic embedded in your existing applications. This logic may help you determine product recommendations in your call center, or it may deal with insurance regulations, pricing, or eligibility.

Changing a rule

Business rules may change often — much more often than your applications or processes do. If the rules are buried in your applications, they're pretty tough to change, and making a change in a business rule could take six months or more based on your application development cycle. Your business can't wait that long, can it?

To get back to the ballgame example (see the preceding section), maybe you got soaked by rain at the game last weekend, and now you want to add a decision criterion so you don't go to the game when it's likely to rain. So you change your rule to add a rain criterion:

> IF 2 adjacent tickets are available to the game in section 103, 104, 105 for less than $50 per ticket
>
> AND IF the chance of precipitation is less than 30%
>
> AND IF no relatives are visiting on the day of the game
>
> AND IF the low temperature on the day of the game is not less than 40°F
>
> THEN buy tickets to the game

Weekends just got better!

Making regular changes

Imagine that you make one or two changes to your rules every month. The rule was fine to start with, but after ten rounds of changes, it's much better, really reflecting the best practices of your company or organization.

Rules are hard to get perfect on the first try, which is why many of your applications aren't as smart as they could be or should be. But when they're done right, they accurately reflect how your business does business.

Stepping through the Rulemaking Process

Rulemaking activities break down into a set of logical steps. We walk you through the process in this section.

Step 1: Decide what changes to make

Something is prompting a change. Perhaps your experts have spotted a way to give the competition a beating, or the market landscape has shifted, or a particular product line is going gangbusters. It could be that your compliance officer has been reviewing your operational procedures and found that you aren't conforming to the latest regulatory changes. Or maybe your analytical whiz kids are looking at historical trends and have anticipated some new trend. Whatever the driver for change is, you need to change your operational decision-making as soon as possible. You may have to alter a current rule, such as a rate calculation, or create a new one to help with decisions such as the optimal deal to offer a prospective client.

Step 2: Find relevant existing rules

In setting up your ODM environment, you established a library of groups and sets of rules covering your operational decisions. Users want to see what rules already exist within the specific area; then they can see which rules may need to be changed and where to add new rules. But even if you don't remember where in the library the rule was stored, you can use search terms and filters, just like in a web search engine, to find all the rules that match your criteria.

Step 3: Discuss and collaborate on the potential changes

When the rules to be changed or created have been identified, the ODM collaboration tools come to the fore. Your users may want to discuss proposed changes with other experts to refine their thinking.

Collaboration has several important side effects:

- When users consult other experts and take their views into account, delivering a high-quality result is easier.

- Identifying the last person who changed a rule can be useful, because he or she may have helpful information to offer.
- It provides a written record not only of when and by whom the rule was changed but also *why* it was changed.

Without in-context collaboration, communication about changes to a specific rule would take place in voicemails or e-mails that wouldn't be maintained in the rule history for future reference.

Step 4: Write or edit a rule

When your business users decide what changes are required and the best ways to make them, they can use the ODM authoring environment to write new rules or edit existing ones. The rules library and ODM search tools are invaluable for this purpose; the rule author can pull up the current copy of the rule, see who changed it last, and review any documentation.

Sometimes, instead of creating a new rule from scratch, it may be productive to use an existing rule as a starting point. If your company is just starting to do business in Austria, for example, you may require a specific set of rules to govern your operations there, but those rules are probably going to look a lot like the ones you currently use in Germany. Simply call up the German set of rules and make just those changes that reflect the differences in doing business in Austria.

Step 5: Simulate and test the rule

Because changing the rules that control your decisions has such an effect on operations, you need to be sure that your changes are going to work.

ODM solutions offer several ways to simulate and test your changes, including running new rules against historical information to see what happens. Although this simulation can never be 100 percent accurate in predicting future performance, it should provide some rapid and valuable feedback on the changes, allowing the rule editors to refine those changes if they don't behave as planned.

It's extremely important to make sure that the changes you're testing don't get deployed without proper approvals into a live production system. ODM provides full governance capabilities to help keep you safe.

Step 6: Deploy the change

After your business users use ODM to find the rules that need to be changed, kick some ideas around with colleagues, make the changes, and validate them against historical data, the next step is introducing the changes to your business operations.

Despite the need for agility in responding to market changes, you also have to ensure stability in your operations. You don't want just anyone changing your business without proper authorization. The ODM software interacts with your security systems to enable you to control the deployment process, ensuring that the correct authorizations and approvals are in place and also preserving an audit trail (see Chapter 3).

Assuming that the changes pass all the checks-and-balances tests, they're ready to be deployed.

Step 7: Monitor and report on the change

At this point, you may want to monitor the new decisions and changes to see how they behave in production as opposed to in the simulation environment. While reporting isn't necessary for all rules, it's a good way to verify that the changes produced the expected results.

The best judges of whether a rule change works are the business users who created that change in the first place. ODM reporting tools can deliver measurement and performance information in user-friendly fashion, presenting the information in a way that's easy to understand and digest.

Reporting also allows you to collect new business performance information for study by your expert analysts. Feedback from production operations is precisely the sort of input that produces maximum benefits for your business operations; business analysts can discuss new changes to make things even better, continually improving your business performance.

Chapter 5

Getting Started with ODM

In This Chapter

- Writing your first rule
- Deploying your rules into ODM
- Discovering existing rules

The beautiful thing about getting started with ODM is that you can do it at your own pace. At its core, ODM is a system for externalizing business rules from your existing applications and processes. Unlike many other types of IT systems, ODM doesn't require a "big bang" approach. By its very nature, it's incremental.

What do we mean by saying that implementing ODM is incremental? Suppose that you have an application containing 5,000 business rules, and about 1,000 of those rules need some flexibility built in. You may need to change those 1,000 rules more frequently than the other rules, or you may need to change them at different times from when you make changes in the application. Perhaps the rules need to be read and modified by a wider group of people — both business and IT users — than is currently possible, or you need additional governance or auditability for the rules.

In this chapter you discover the process for creating rules in ODM and how rules are tested, deployed, invoked, and changed.

Replicating a Rule

Getting started is easy. You import your data model (or create a new data model for importation, if necessary) into an ODM system and then replicate one of those 1,000 existing rules.

You don't change it yet; you merely replicate it in ODM. The process doesn't take long because you don't have to write the entire rule yourself — the ODM system provides a lot of help. Drop-down menus list options based on the data model you imported and the actions available at every point in the rule. Autocompletion make the process easy, and consistency checking alerts you to any potential problem. We've seen businesspeople who've never been exposed to an ODM tool create a good rule in the first ten minutes.

Testing the Replicated Rule

The next step is testing the replicated rule, using the ODM tool's built-in testing function. As with any other automated function, you need to create some test cases for which you already know the answer. Testing can be done in a spreadsheet that's set up to show you which test cases passed and which (if any) failed. For any failures, you check the rule to see where it didn't mirror your intent. Based on what you find, make changes and retest the rule until it passes.

Deploying the Rule

Your next step is deploying the rule to the ODM runtime engine (see Chapter 3) — a high-performance, highly scalable environment that can accurately execute thousands of rules per second (assuming you have the appropriate IT infrastructure in place).

Calling the Rule

The final step of the process is calling the rule from the application or process. Now, whenever the application needs to invoke this business rule, instead of invoking the logic inside the application, it invokes the business rule in the external ODM application.

Changing the Rule

Suppose that this rule pertains to eligibility requirements. Two weeks from now, your company's policy on eligibility changes, meaning that you have to change that business rule. Instead of making changes in the application, which could take many months, you simply make changes to the business rule in the ODM system. Even with the necessary governance, simulation, and testing, it's reasonable to think that you could deploy the new rule in one or two weeks. (You could deploy it even more rapidly if the necessary approvers are poised and ready to respond quickly.) The result: You've added value to your organization by changing the implementation of a business policy quickly and flexibly.

Discovering Existing Rules

Where are your current business rules? While they may be in many places, one way to approach the question is to think in terms of two types of rules:

1. Those that are currently codified into an application or process
2. Those that aren't codified and that are in documents, spreadsheets, or the heads of your business experts

REMEMBER

One of the key ways that ODM helps is through the collaboration and versioning features, so your team can work together to document and iteratively improve your organization's rules. In this rule discovery process, it's often helpful to use a dedicated, web-based collaboration tool as a platform for sharing ideas and zeroing in on specific rules you want to automate and how they should be expressed. You don't have to deploy all your rules at once; you can roll them out in waves, starting with the ones that will have the most business impact.

Chapter 6

Ten ODM Use Cases

In This Chapter

- Understanding how ODM helps repeatable decisions
- Looking at proven starting points for ODM

A lot of your business involves repeatable decisions, many of which you may want to improve. Some may be automated but hard to change. Others may be automated but not as well as you want. Yet others may not be automated at all. If you think your operational decisions may be good candidates for ODM, this chapter gives you ten proven entry points to help you get started.

Credit and Loan Approvals

A generation ago, lenders were in the driver's seat. A borrower went through the painful exercise of applying for a loan, hoping that the lender would approve. Today's borrowers make five online loan applications before breakfast, and although they may not get approval by lunch, lenders will be fighting for their business by dinner.

Many loan decisions (both consumer and commercial) are based on or at least influenced by the speed at which lenders can grant approval. Yet as we've seen over the past few years, inappropriate loan decisions can have disastrous results. At the same time, regulatory issues and fairness concerns put pressure on financial institutions to be consistent and auditable in their credit and loan approvals.

ODM provides a way to automate much of the credit and loan approval process. It can improve straight-through processing, send exception cases to experienced loan officers, and provide an audit trail of all loan decisions that were made and the specific rules that were applied.

Claims Processing

Business rules can help you manage much of the complexity of claims processing. The rules may be different for every state or region. Coverage may differ depending on the details of a medical or dental procedure. Workers' compensation and social services claims may have a very different set of processing requirements. Although ODM can't automate all claims processing, it can free skilled employees to work on only those claims that require special attention.

Underwriting

Assigning risk is a risky endeavor. Price too low, and you lose money. Price too high, and you lose business. And if you take too long to price a policy, a loan, or anything else, you may lose the business because your potential customer found another provider.

Underwriting involves a great deal of knowledge and data. As mysterious as this expertise can sometimes seem, it can be quantified, which makes it a perfect candidate for business rules. ODM can help you automate most of your underwriting decisions without sacrificing quality.

Compliance and Reporting

Compliance is all about rules, so it makes sense that ODM is the perfect technology to automate it. No matter what type of regulations you're complying with, an easy-to-use, easy-to-change rule management system can greatly simplify the process, especially if you have a complex matrix of regulations to deal with, with different regulations in each state or region. ODM can also help you speed the reporting process so that many reports can be generated in real or near real time.

Dynamic Pricing and Bundling

Dynamic pricing and bundling strategies are often the best ways to find the "sweet spot" that enables you to make the sale and make a profit at the same time. The perfect price today may not be the perfect price next week, after all. Your suppliers may be charging more, your competitors may be lowering their prices, or your demand may be changing.

Coming up with a pricing policy that keeps pace with a constantly shifting market is difficult, but so is continuously updating your IT systems to reflect those changes. ODM provides a perfect vehicle for maintaining the rules that dictate your dynamic pricing and bundling.

Fraud Detection

Business rules can easily apply hundreds of validation criteria to reduce the chances of fraud. In a medical claim, for example, you can verify whether a certain procedure is valid for the specific combination of patient, doctor, and hospital. By adding predictive analytics, you can look for hidden patterns and rank them in order of likely fraudulence.

REMEMBER

Although no system can detect all possible fraud, ODM can automate the process of finding inconsistencies that may indicate fraud.

Eligibility Determination

Eligibility rules may be complex, there may be a lot of them, and they may differ across geographic borders, but at the end of the day, they're just rules. ODM provides a tailor-made environment that allows business users or IT personnel to update rules frequently and to implement fully governed changes in days or weeks instead of months.

Cross-Sell, Upsell, and Product Recommendations

The art and science of making good product recommendations is still relatively young, but businesses are constantly improving their capability to make customized recommendations to individual customers. Whether the recommendations are made by customer-service reps over the phone, in an office, or online, advances in technology and personalization enable you to get recommendations right more often and increase the odds that customers will be interested in those products. ODM, along with analytics, helps you harness information to increase the effectiveness of your product recommendations.

Customer Loyalty Programs

You'd think that a good loyalty program would have no downside, but many consumers are leaving these programs. Many of the businesses who run loyalty programs really don't know their customers, so they offer low-value incentives, impersonal engagements, and irrelevant promotions and messages. Sometimes, they even promote merchandise that customers have already bought and are unlikely to need again.

You don't have to be one of those businesses. ODM can help you ensure that the promotions and messages you send to your customers are relevant so that your loyalty program keeps those customers satisfied and engaged.

Customs and Border Control

Countries need to monitor and control the inflow of people and goods across their borders without slowing that movement to a crawl. Business rules can quickly evaluate thousands of relevant criteria pertaining to security risks and customs declarations. ODM systems can prescreen travelers and goods before they reach the border and evaluate border security and customs declarations in near real time. ODM also enables rules to be updated easily, yet safely, so that changes in border regulations can be enacted quickly.

Chapter 7

Ten Characteristics of Best-in-Class ODM Systems

In This Chapter

- Understanding why ODM is more than a rules engine
- Looking at how business events provide real-time inputs
- Seeing the complementary solutions to ODM

At this point, you may think that ODM is a cool business solution, but you may wonder if it makes sense to introduce another piece of software into your organization because IT already has too much complexity. What we've found with our clients, however, is that ODM actually reduces complexity and makes it easier for organizations to adapt to change by providing a balance of freedom and governance. In this chapter, we look at a few reasons why organizations invest in ODM.

Management Capabilities

The key word here is *management.* ODM implementations can have anywhere from a few hundred rules to 100,000 rules or more. The management part of operational decision management enables you to organize, track, catalog, change, govern, simulate, test, audit, reuse, search for, collaborate on, and report on your business rules and operational decisions. Essentially, it means that an organized system is in place to manage the entire life cycle of all the rules in your enterprise, whether you're on your first project or your twentieth.

Notice that we don't mention rule authoring and execution here. Those functions, although absolutely necessary, are just the beginning. A decision engine is also an important part of the solution, but (to use a car analogy) most of us wouldn't buy an engine that didn't have a good vehicle around it. You might say that ODM attaches a transmission, odometer, brakes, headlights, seats, and seatbelts to your decision engine.

Less Reliance on IT

Business rules represent the business policies, regulations, and best practices related to your business. These rules have too great an effect on the business for you to keep them locked in systems that only IT personnel can access or read.

We're not advocating that IT step out of the way and not be involved. Given resource constraints and the speed at which change needs to take place, however, a partnership between business and IT makes sense. Most IT departments would like to conserve resources by allowing business users to make routine changes to business rules, assuming that those changes are made in a safe environment with the right checks and balances.

By providing the necessary checks and balances, ODM enables business users to assume much of the responsibility for day-to-day rule changes. It's a win-win situation, significantly reducing IT's workload while enabling business policy changes to be made much more quickly and accurately.

Intuitive Interface

Business people today expect tools to be intuitive, partly because everyone is busy, but also because consumer electronics companies have trained us to expect intuitive interfaces. The need for intuitive interfaces extends to IT personnel, who like elegant, intuitive interfaces that don't force them to keep checking the user manual or online help.

Business Events Capabilities

An ODM system can listen for specific events — a bank-machine withdrawal, a location change based on GPS or another positioning system, or a person visiting a web page. The ODM system can not only track these events but also correlate groups of events to identify patterns. A credit card company, for example, might be interested to know that John Doe used his credit card on two continents within an hour. An insurance company might like to know that three car insurance applications were submitted in the past 72 hours for the same vehicle but at different addresses.

Rules that govern business events can play a pivotal role in an ODM system. When you determine that an event (or group of events) of interest has taken place, you can use business rules to decide what response is appropriate and to initiate action.

This process is often referred to as Detect–Decide–Act. Business events enable you to *detect* a certain situation in real time; the associated business rules enable you to *decide* the appropriate response and then *act.*

Built-in Governance and Change Management

We know that governance isn't the most exciting topic, but it's a crucial part of ODM. You'll be using ODM to automate your corporate policies and regulations, so you need a clear, easy-to-use way to ensure that proper approvals have been granted for each new or updated rule.

One key advantage of ODM is that it provides a structured governance model, because your rules are stored and managed in a dedicated system and aren't intertwined into your applications and processes.

Another important aspect of business rule governance is change management. The central repository in ODM is able to provide user-friendly change management and version control that differentiates among prior versions of a rule, the current version of the rule in production, and the proposed new version of the rule that's in the process of going through approval. The change management system can also store work-in-progress drafts of future proposed versions of the rule — for example, pricing and bundling rules for an upcoming holiday promotion.

Centralized, Searchable Rules Repository

An ODM system should provide a repository that's centralized from the start and that's easy to manage and search. Search capabilities should be on a par with the top search engines on the web.

A good search function is the best way to promote reuse. An insurance company, for example, may want to see whether any existing rules apply to sports cars in California. An ODM search should be able to provide a list of rules that have the words *sports car* or *California* in the title, body, or metadata within seconds, even when the repository contains 30,000 rules.

The search tool should be able to easily filter by parameters, such as business rules or decision tables. It also should be able to search by criteria such as rule status (in production or preproduction) or when the rule was last modified.

Integrated Simulation and Testing

An important benefit of ODM is simulation capability. Assuming that you're trying to maximize profit, you want to answer questions about the effect of a price change before you implement the change, rather than later. ODM systems provide a user-friendly but powerful way to run simulations. You can simulate not only against sample data, but also last week's or last month's data to see what results you would have had in the real world with a different set of rules.

Testing is also an important part of a successful ODM solution, and it should be as easy to accomplish as possible. An ODM system should be able to create a spreadsheet to facilitate testing and to display test results visually, for example.

Auditing and Reporting

Imagine how nice it would be to be able to trace the life cycle of a decision quickly and easily. That's part of what ODM offers: a decision warehouse that provides easy access to all that information. If you need to look back ten years in time, the decision warehouse enables you to go to any information in your ODM deployment and generate the necessary reports.

You have a history of who wrote and approved each rule, as well as a record of all the posted comments about that rule. Then, at runtime, you can easily trace any automated decision to see why it was made. The decision warehouse shows you the rules that were in place when the decision was executed and why the decision conformed to the business rules that were in effect at the time.

Reuse of Rules

As you improve business rules over time, you create valuable enterprise assets because your rules represent how your business does business. As rules become optimized, their reuse becomes increasingly valuable. Reuse can take place not only across multiple applications and business processes but also across channels. The same rule can be called by web applications, mobile applications, and call-center applications, for example.

Reuse across applications, processes, and channels can greatly increase your consistency in business operations and customer service; at the same time, it reduces the resources you need to develop applications, processes, and business rules.

Easy Integration with Other Solutions

ODM complements virtually every type of business and technology solution, but a few solutions integrate especially well with ODM:

- *Business Process Management* (BPM) is the best solution for managing processes that take place over time. Processes managed by BPM may take anywhere from a few minutes to a few months (or longer in some cases). ODM, on the other hand, manages decisions that are made at a specific point in time. Although ODM technically has a concept of flow, that flow takes place in milliseconds, and the end-user isn't aware of it. By contrast, BPM is best at managing flows that take anywhere from minutes to months. Working together, the two technologies are a natural pair, with BPM providing the long-running solution and ODM making the specific operational decisions.

- *Business analytics* is another key capability that works hand in hand with ODM, allowing you to base your decisions both on what you know (such as business practices, policies, and regulations) and on what you can predict.

  Typically, you have two ways to create joint operational and analytical solutions: one in which the analytics are used at design time and one in which analytics are calculated at runtime. In the design-time method, analytics are used to create business rules for use by ODM. At the time they're invoked, these rules may be anywhere from days to months old. The method is good for rules that don't rely on real-time information from other systems, such as a rule that predicts the occurrence of rare diseases when patients are admitted to a hospital. The rule might say, "If the patient has x symptom and y symptom, there is a xx% likelihood that he or she has z disease."

  By contrast, a rule that requires near real-time inputs from other systems would be one that predicts the likelihood of default on a loan. The decision would depend on recent updates, such as adverse credit or risk information made available in the past few days or hours.

- *Enterprise Service Bus* (ESB) is an integration bus that serves as the core of most systems based on service-oriented architecture. This integration method provides message routing and transformation, among other services. This routing and transformation can be programmed into the ESB itself but is subject to the same limitations as business rules that are hidden in applications. It's much more effective to externalize these business rules in ODM to provide the same benefits that ODM provides to other applications.